Swir

MW01282251

using the 4-hour chart

Part 3: Where Do I Put My stop?

Heikin Ashi Trader

BOOK DESCRIPTION

In the third part of the series on "Swing Trading using the 4-hour chart", the Heikin Ashi Trader treats the question on where the stop should be. Once a trader stops introducing stops, he will discover that his hit rate will worsen. However, by doing this he gains full control of the trade management. Stops are therefore not unavoidable, but remain an integral part of a trading system that is profit-oriented.

Well understood stops are downright the actual instrument that makes profit possible. Since money is only earned when he exits the trade, the trader should try to perform the stop management with the utmost care. The formulation of crystal-clear rules, both for trend trades as well as for trades with a fixed target, after all, is the requirement to ensure that the trader is playing his own game.

Every successful trader has ultimately developed his own rules. No matter what the market does, this trader always plays his own game and can be swayed by anything. Precisely the persistence and consistency with which he operates in the market ensures that he becomes one day the "Master of the Game".

Table of Contents

ARE STOPS NECESSARY?

Where do I put my stop? Many traders ask me this question repeatedly. This often sounds a bit like an annoying accessory about which the trader has to worry still, after doing the important work of market analysis and after the trader has already bought the position. The question touches on the most important issue, which a trader may and must ask himself: How much risk am I willing to take in order to buy me the next chance?

Unfortunately, behind this question mostly, a childish desire is hidden whether I might reveal to the budding trader a kind of hideout, where he can put in this annoying thing, called "Stop", so Mr. Market can never find it. Curiously, Mr. Market has a good nose for such hiding places, especially if the stop is located just below or above striking marks such as support and resistance. How this happens, was the subject of the second book in this series on swing trading.

Stops are a controversial topic in trading circles. No wonder, because stops belong to the exit strategy of a trading system. In other words, a stop is the central risk management tool and therefore directly has to do with making money in the stock market. It is therefore imperative that you understand which function the stop has in your trading system or in your strategy.

It must be clear to you from the outset that the use of stops always results in a lower hit rate. If you trade without stops, you will probably reach a very high hit rate. However, you might wait sometimes for a very long time before some positions go into profit. In addition, some positions never will and you would be forced to close these trades with very high losses.

If the trader uses stops, he might avoid such a scenario. In return, he has to accept losing trades quite more often. Those losing trades are the price you are willing to pay in order to control the risk. You cannot do this when you trade without stops. In this case, your risk is unlimited.

If you chose to trade with stops - and I urge you to do so -, the hit rate of your system will automatically deteriorate. You will not win in 100% of the cases, but in only 70% or 60% or even lower. There are even very successful strategies that work very well with very low hit rates.

This is for example; usually the case for trend followers. Here, the trader must often make multiple attempts to establish a position in a trend. This naturally leads to many small losses and a few big winners. The result might be positive, but the trader must sometimes accept a hit rate that is below 30%.

Of course, a high hit rate strokes the ego, for which many beginners desire this, eagerly. To achieve this goal, many of them then take the risk to trade without stops. When the first truly great losses occur, the insight may grow to use stops.

This does not mean that this trader really accepted stops. He accepts them with a certain bad mood. You will notice this mostly because he does everything so that the stop is not reached. Often than not, those same traders realize some little profit as soon as they can see it. Better a small profit in your pocket than nothing, they say.

All these bad habits are a consequence of the non-acceptance of stops. The trader uses them though, mostly because he was forced to, but in his mind, he hates stops because they inevitably lead to losing trades, repeatedly.

Only gradually, the insight ripens that trading has precious little to do with "wanting to always be right on the market". Trading is a business like any other. That is, there are earnings and expenses and hopefully the earnings are higher than the expenses at the end of the fiscal year. That is, the art of managing a business is to keep costs as low as possible and to optimize the earnings or increase them through business expansion.

It is no different to when trading. Since trading is a business, there are earnings (winning trades) and costs (loss trades, commissions, hardware, space rent and hourly wage of the trader). Since the losing trades represent most of the costs, we speak also rightly of "costs of doing business". In other words, losing trades are part of our main costs. They are necessary so that we can attend in-market activity.

Whoever understands losing trades as simple "cost" so that you can participate in the economic game or the stock market game, perhaps begins to realize that losing trades are not such bad things at all that you would prefer to banish from your trading life.

On the contrary: they are the condition to be able to participate, and thus is an integral part of our trading system. Our trading system would therefore be ridiculous without losing trades.

Therefore, it would be a completely absurd measure to want to banish them from it.

Once the trader has internalized this idea, then the next step is not far to understand trading as a kind of probability game, which it is. Similar to the entrepreneur in the retail sector, who is of course concerned about quality, but tries by a certain pricing policy to keep his costs as low as possible.

Similarly, the trader should do everything he can to keep his losses as small as possible. Furthermore, I will go into this in the first part of this book. In addition, of course, the second part will be about how stops can help us to maximize our profits, because they actually can.

Therefore, a real trader looks at the stop order not as unavoidable, but as his friend, standing beside him in the management of his positions. That it is also the attitude of a professional or institutional trader requires no further explanation, hopefully.

WHAT IS A STOP LOSS ORDER?

A stop loss order (also; order to limit losses) is an order that automatically closes the position when a certain price is reached. If a trader accompanies a purchased position (or a selling position for short positions) by a stop-loss order, he thus reflects that he will not accept an unlimited loss that may be associated with the position.

This measure belongs to the good trading habits and I recommend each trader develop this habit in order to operate this business for the long term. One might consider the stop as a kind of a natural instinct of the trader. Ultimately, the survival instinct is present with almost every individual. This applies above all to responsible traders who should see it as their primary task to protect and obtain the trading capital.

The **stop-loss order** means nothing else than that a contract, a stock or a currency pair is sold at the next tradable price once the market reaches a pre-set price level. With the simple stop Loss an unlimited market sell order will be generated (in the case of a long position).

Some brokers also offer **stop-loss limit orders**. In this case, the position will be sold only at the specified limit price. This can be an advantage in some cases, because with the simple stop loss, the position is often sold at a worse price than the price the stop loss order displays.

However, the disadvantage of this stop-loss limit order outweighs the advantage by far. In the worst case, the market overruns in one quick move the fixed limit, and there is no execution. In this case, the position is exposed to unlimited risk, a condition every trader should avoid at all costs.

Some brokers also offer **guaranteed stop loss orders**. The broker guarantees to close the position exactly to the desired price. Therefore, he reflects the offsetting risk and assumes the costs for the case that the execution was far below or above the targeted stop price. This may, in rare cases be an advantage for the trader, especially when it comes to extreme movements in the market.

This "service" is, of course, not free of cost. Either usually the customer pays for this service a small fee, or the broker demands a wider spread (larger distance between the purchase and selling price). In addition, the trader will have to accept a greater distance between the entry price and the stop to get a guaranteed stop loss order.

Though this additional security usually might not be an option for day traders and scalpers, it might be a sensible alternative that is worth pondering for swing traders who often hold trades for several days and weeks.

As a swing trader, it is usually not a question of whether you buy the EUR/USD at 1.1210 or 1.1212. Of course, 1.1210 is a better price if you want to buy. But if I can sleep on both ears because my broker pays the difference, should it come to an extreme overnight move in the EUR/USD or at the weekend, then I am willing to pay a worse price.

STOP MANAGEMENT

I want to cover in this third part of the series "Swing Trading with the 4-hour Chart" the central theme of the stop-management itself, because this is what ultimately decides whether a trading business is successful or not. It is well known that private investors 90% of the time are engaged in market analysis, and not even 10% of the time with the question of the potential risk of a trade.

For institutional traders this ratio is reversed. Professionals are inherently primarily risk managers. They have to be, because their customers and financiers are there immediately if they feel that the fund in which they have invested, is not even in a position to preserve its capital, let alone grow.

Now, the trading capital of a private investor is usually more manageable than the capital of an institutional investor, who often uses complex risk models to manage the customer's money. Hence, to conclude that a private trader with the simple 1% rule has done enough of risk management seems to me to be thinking a little too short.

The 1% rule states that a trader should never risk more than 1% of his capital per trade. If a trader, for example, has $10,000 available capital to trade with, the risk per trade should never be more than $100. This seems to be obvious, but still leads past the actual topic.

The ability to calculate correctly the distance between the purchase price and the stop is important; it is but only the beginning of the process, which I call stop management. This in turn is an important part of the exit strategy, the final arbiter of success or failure in the stock market. Moreover, here regrettably, the private investor is subject mostly to the experienced professional.

Professionals usually have sophisticated and accurately defined exit strategies. Private investors mostly act quite emotionally with this subject. If the position is in the win, they like to take this gain, although there might be often no objective reason to do this.

If the position is and remains in the loss and even approaches the stop-loss order, amateurs usually remain passive and fall into the well-known "hope" mode: the "market" could turn again. Thus, they give the monster they call "market", an infinite power over them, as if they were exposed to it unconditionally.

Whoever takes a closer look at this behavior (I belonged to this group myself for years), notes that most private traders attach far too much importance to the so-called "market" (and its analysis). For them this elusive phenomenon called "market" seems to be an indomitable monster to which they appear to be delivered completely. Recriminations and even anger are feelings that can arise very quickly from such an attitude. I know this too well, when I look back on my rookie season.

The miserable treatment, not to say **the non-existence of an exit strategy** is the proof that most traders go into the stock market with the intention to be slaughtered. That sounds dramatic, but it corresponds to the inner attitude of many, which is unfortunately confirmed by the success statistics. No one knows the numbers exactly, but whoever believes that 90% of traders lose, belongs to the most incorrigible optimists.

Brokers incidentally do not like to get out with those numbers. When questioned with a little pressure, you usually get vague answers. "We do not have statistics on this issue" is still one of the more harmless variants of their excuses. It is understandable that they are very reluctant. Any form of transparency in this regard hurts their business.

The real number of losers might probably approach the 100 % level, particularly with the forex brokers. In the long term, only a percentage of traders who will probably be found in the parts per thousand ranges seem to survive. Why is this so? Why is the trading business so difficult and only a tiny group of people seemed to have lasting success?

Most traders fail to themselves. As often is the analysis. Most people psychologically, are not prepared or trained enough to meet this challenge. The many losses repeatedly coming up and the drawdown phases (loss rows) wear down eventually the psyche of Traders. He begins to make mistakes; he takes too many risks to make up for the losses and in this way makes everything worse. One day the money is simply gone.

I certainly am among those who welcome the psychological argument. It is true that most traders fail to themselves. There is a lack of discipline, consistency and perseverance. There is a lack of almost everything really. However, above all, there is a severe lack of insight on what trading actually is: a probability game.

In my view, this aspect is somewhat underexposed in the relevant literature. In recent years, many trading coaches have emerged that do a good job with in-depth knowledge of psychology. In addition, as a trader if you have the feeling that you might have deficits here, I can only recommend that you be trained by a trading Coach.

I will not go into this subject in this book. I will like to introduce more of a risk model that allows the trader to run his stop management efficiently. This model also suits the idea that trading is a probability game indeed.

PLAY YOUR OWN GAME

Each trading strategy is based on certain assumptions on how the financial markets work, and how to operate in them as a trader. These assumptions can be formulated explicitly, or implicitly underpinning the strategy is based. A trader, who choses trend following as his core strategy, bases his work on the explicit assumption that most markets move in long-lasting trends. If you feel this way, then it is only logical that you will try to follow those trends as long as possible.

Behind this specific market, acceptance is but still a (mostly unconscious) layer, of which I am of the opinion that it is worthwhile to look at this in more detail. This layer touches the theme of "success" centrally, and anyone who had only approximately dealt with success literature, will be addressing this issue.

All success coaches stress over the importance of the right mindset you must have to succeed. It is all about the way we think about the world and, consequently, how we view the world. In trading terms, the worldview of most traders looks like this: out there, there are tens of thousands of other traders who are all my opponents and who have only one thing on their mind: to get at my money.

This model seems banal, but it is the basic assumption of most traders I know. For them the world is (the world outside of themselves) a hostile place you can conquer only by clever tactics, to secure a piece of the cake.

In this model, so there is an "I" (the trader), which goes into the world (operating on the stock exchange) in the hope that by clever and skillful conduct he can steer a portion of the cash flow to his own account. Consequently, the trader who thinks so is always in a kind of defense mode. His actions are always reactive. If the market (the outside world) does this, he reacts like that. The market does that, he reacts like this.

He is, as if in a constant struggle with a fictitious opponent, he does not even know. He only sees his tracks as lines or candles, the chart drawn in front of his eyes on the monitor.

This model corresponds to a thinking that turns the world into a subject-object reality. On the one hand there is the "I" which identifies a trader that goes into the "world" to make conquests there in the hope of returning home with a fat booty.

This model corresponds to the assumptions of the classical sciences on which ultimately our modern societies are built. It is the way we have been brought up in school and therefore determines massively the way how we look at "the world".

Now, I am the last person who would argue that this model is wrong. On the contrary, it is very real and determines our lives in almost all areas. The only problem is that this mode of thinking is not very useful if we operate on the stock market. Because, if you act on the stock exchange with this rational, you will quickly (often unconsciously) see yourself as a victim of higher powers, when things are not going as well as you had hoped.

It is imperative that as a trader you never take the position of a "victim". On the contrary, as a trader, you should always have full control over your actions. You should from the beginning be "the Master of the Game" and stay there.

In order to achieve this quality you will need a different philosophy, a different way of thinking, which corresponds to the circumstances of a probability game. Because trading has – I have to say it very clearly - nothing to do with exchange rates, central banks, hedge funds, algorithms and whatever else your brain likes to invent about what everything is "out there".

Trading is a game that you play only with yourself. I repeat this sentence: **Trading is a game you play with yourself**. Trading is nothing more than a series of transactions that you perform on your own, self-imposed rules on the market.

In other words: If you see trading like this, you have the better advantage that you are the one who makes the rules even before the game starts. You may choose the means by which the game is to be performed. In addition, - finally yet importantly - you can determine when the game starts and when it ends!

Have you ever seen or experienced such advantages in a board game with friends? Probably not. For among friends they all have the same opportunities early in the game. If you need to compete do it with your friends in a social gathering, on the stock market you have no competitors. You can decide how or what you want to play, how often and when the game is over. Have you ever experienced such advantages?

Yet, most people who go to the stock market lose, despite this huge advantage. Isn´t that incredible?

You can only win this game if you also believe that you play with yourself and with your own rules. Only then, will you experience success if you are convinced that you are all alone and there is nobody there, who prevents your success. Do you have that conviction?

I had this conviction as a child. In the basement of our house, we had a table football game. Whenever I was bored, I descended into the cellar and played with myself. I chose a fictitious enemy, against whom I wanted to play. I needed a fictitious enemy; otherwise, the game would have been boring. Then I started to play. Now and then, I let my opponents score a goal, so my game stayed exciting, but in the end, I always won the game. I always won, because I, and only I, made the rules. Do you understand?

It is the same when you go to the stock exchange. Try to do it just like the child I once was. Tell yourself: I am starting now to play, but first I make the rules. After all, you are "the Master of the Game".

The rules that you have thought up, of course, are based on certain assumptions that you have made before the game starts. Because you only need a small, "statistical" advantage to be able to win the game in the long term. If you have not previously installed this small statistical advantage in your rules, you cannot win your own game. Then you have beaten yourself so to speak.

Casino operators know this as well. The statistical advantage of a casino is 1%. This seems tiny, but it is enough to the casino to make millions of profit every year. Year for year. Casino operators know that they lose in 49% of the cases against their clients. You can see them leaving the casino with a beaming smile on their face and a fat cigar.

However, the casino operator who observes on the cameras the bustle of his customers, and sees the jackpot winner leaving the building with his cigar is also smiling. Because he knows that for every jackpot winner there are thousands of losers who wash money in his treasury on a daily basis. Thanks to the small statistical advantage, he remains the "Master of the Game". After all, he is the one who is pocketing a very rich booty at the end of the fiscal year and not the cigar smoker.

As a trader, you should familiarize yourself with the mentality and thinking of a casino operator. You should say: Be it from time to time somebody is leaving the house with a fat cigar, I will be winning at the end of the day, because I;

A. Understand the game because I designed it myself.
B. I always win the game because I have installed a small statistical advantage in the rules.

Who goes with such thinking and such a mentality to the stock market? Who can beat this man (this woman)? Nobody! Because this person has no opponent but himself. But since this person knows very well his opponent (namely himself) and therefore formulated very clear rules by which he plays and by which he can outsmart himself, this person wins time and time again. He may have weak days, but in the end, he has mastered the game that he designed himself and wins.

Now do you understand why it is so important to formulate clear entry and exit rules before you even start? These must then be performed in a disciplined way during the game. Without these rules, you will never succeed because then you let "others" enter YOUR game which will in turn cause you to fail. It is therefore imperative that you establish yourself, your own trading philosophy, in which only you are the owner of the game, the only player, and finally the one who comes out victorious in the end.

Nobody should get involved therefore, no matter what may happen on your charts. This is all much less important than you think. The bottom line is that you always play your game and never move away from that.

Nevertheless, in order to play YOUR game, you must have developed a game in the first place, which looks like a game. In addition, I hereby claim that just over 90% of the traders do not own their own game.

To say: I trade this or that setup, place my stop so that I lose only 1%, and take a profit as soon as I feel that it is enough. That is you will hopefully realize not a single game.

For a real trading game that you develop for yourself must be described and formulated that you can actually show it one day to your friends.

Your friends will only be able to play it with you when the rules are formulated clear, preferably written clearly on a piece of paper, so that each participant can read and understand it. If there is only one obscurity or an interpretable rule, your friends may refuse to play the game with you. They will tell you: Oh let us return to the game from last week and play that. Here the rules are clear and everyone knows them. Thus, there is no strife.

Can you see it? Therefore, it should be. As long as you do not have clearly defined and formulated such a game for yourself, you do not know what you are doing. You are then simply doing transactions in the stock market.

That may have a certain appeal for some beginners, especially if they have never done it and when your own money is at stake. However, eventually you will realize that only "performing transactions on the stock market" does not necessarily have the consequence that you actually make money.

Any form of making money ALWAYS has to do with a kind of statistical advantage, no matter what game you dream up. In addition, most of all, it has to do with clearly pre-defined rules. I want to illustrate this based on a known example in order for you to accurately understand what I mean.

Everyone knows the coffee house chain **Starbucks**. No wonder, because Starbucks is represented almost all over the world and the chain often has several branches in larger cities. Now, Starbucks is certainly not the inventor of the coffee house. Long before Starbucks came into the world, there have been quite beautiful and original coffee houses all over the world. You just need to go to Vienna in Austria, and then you will know what I mean.

Now when Starbucks took over to conquer the world, the makers have not said yes, if we go to Vienna, then we need to set our local branch just in Viennese style, otherwise the people of Vienna will not drink our coffee. In addition, if we go to Paris, we will have to open a cafe in Parisian style. The same is true then just for New York, Seattle or Canberra.

However, if you know Starbucks, then you know that the makers of this chain have not done anything like this. A Starbucks in Vienna, Paris or New York looks just the same as in Brussels, Frankfurt or London. The same varieties will be served, the service people greet you in the same way and the whole cafe works in all 23,768 branches (as of 2016) in the same manner.

As a coffee gourmet you might criticize this, saying the Café Landtmann or the Café Sperl in Vienna is much dearer to me (me too!) Nevertheless, you cannot say that Starbucks is not successful with its strategy. Starbucks is so successful that it has finally become a publicly traded company with a market capitalization of US$ 84 billion.

This is not the case for Café Landtmann and the Café Sperl in Vienna. These traditional cafes are successful in their own way. Landtmann plays just the Landtmann game while Starbucks plays the Starbucks game.

In addition, Starbucks plays this game just the same no matter what, even in Mongolia. It does not matter how the folklore or local circumstances are or which "market conditions" they encounter. Starbucks always plays the game in a "Starbuck's way". Although the local competition is huge sometimes, as in Vienna, which is actually matchless in terms of its coffee houses. Starbucks doesn't care. Starbucks has just not established a Viennese version of Starbucks, not even there (I looked at it) it has the same shape as the Seattle Starbucks.

In other words, Starbucks continues to play its own game, no matter what the circumstances are. As a trader, you should do the same. Every successful trader I know proceeds according to this principle. How different the "methods" of individual traders may be, they play their own game, because they know from experience that they are successful with it.

Now, when so many different traders with so many different methods are successful, then you should finally realize hopefully that market success has absolutely nothing to do with a particular method or strategy, what many beginners seem to believe.

It is true that after a period of trial and error every successful trader has developed his own method that suits his personality. However, he is not successful because of this method. He is successful because he runs his method with a

"Starbucks′″ discipline and tenacity". Moreover, he does this day after day, year after year.

Because he stays with his game and never deviates from it, after a certain time he actually became the "Master of the Game". He has his place in the stock market, which no one would dispute, because only he sits on the throne, no one else.

Therefore, it is unnecessary to copy the method of a master in my view in the hope that the success will also adjust to you. Generally, this will not happen. If you are attempting to copy Starbucks (some companies tried) just because Starbucks is successful, you will fail.

If you understand the Starbucks principle, but you design your own rules that suit you, then you have indeed a chance on the market, as it has been successfully demonstrated by other coffee chains.

Therefore, trading also works. Of course, you can learn from a successful trader. But, you will not learn anything if you merely copy his method and apply it for yourself. You will learn from him if you watch how he plays HIS game every day, no matter what the central banks are doing again, or which disasters may take place in the oil market or in the equity markets. These events are just there to confuse and distract you from your own game.

As long as you can still be distracted, you are still living in the subject-object world, so in the model that has been taught to us in school and universities, namely, that we, when we go out into the world, we will find countless competitors that we must fight, so that we can get a piece of the pie. I will tell you in all clarity: this thinking is pure bullshit.

There is nothing out there. Nothing at all. There is only you and YOUR game. If you do not believe it, try to continue with this old style, I wish you all the luck in the world. I just want to say: in my experience, all successful people on this planet are playing their own game. They have their own rules by which they live, play, and do not give a damn about what others think or say, or what the market dictates to them.

CUT YOUR LOSSES

You will repeatedly encounter the term "free trade" in trading literature. What do I mean by that? It is a position that you have opened, and which is out of the risk. That is, with this trade, you cannot make any more losses, only profits. This situation occurs when you have put your protective stop on cost, so on the price level where you bought it (or sold if you are short).

From that moment, you do not allow the trade to go in to the loss. The worst thing that can happen now is that the market comes back and you are stopped out. However, since your stop is on cost, you will neither win in this case, nor lose. The result is zero.

Now every aspiring trader knows the golden trading rule: **cut your losses, and let your profits run.** It is in every trading book, and everyone takes the sentence as a given. You know it, and that was it.

Hardly anyone looks at this sentence more closely, let alone made every effort to put it into practice. In the portfolios of many investors, positions are sometimes for months or even longer in risk. They have no gains or barely. For out of this minimal profit or minimum loss a great loss can always buildup.

The argument of the proponents of this method is: you have to give the market room to breathe. (Technically speaking, one should take into account the natural volatility of the market and then adjust your stop loss).

For this record sounds the aforementioned victim mentality again. Here someone is just not playing his own game, but leaves it to the "natural fluctuation or volatility" whether and how much he will lose. This mentality is not a favorite of my approach, stating that I determine the rules of the game as a trader and I play exclusively by my rules.

Any experienced trader knows that the longer the trade is in the loss, the less likely it is that it will make him a profit. If this is so, I committed this knowledge to install **a time component in my stop management**. When a position after a certain pre-determined time is not in profit, either the risk must be reduced or the position needs to be closed.

This sounds rigorous, but this measure is consistent with the first part of the golden rule of trading. This says that I should do everything possible to limit the losses. If I know that positions that have not exceeded the breakeven point after a certain time, will not likely, do this in the future, why do I want to maintain this position. It only costs me nerves.

It belongs to the good trading habits to reduce loss positions dramatically or close the same when after a certain time you feel that you are going to lose money.

What time rule applies here?

This depends on the time unit in which you are trading. As a swing trader, who works with a 4-hour chart, then you should not get uneasy after 5 minutes when your position still has not exceeded the breakeven level. If the position after 24 hours (after six candles in the chart) is still a loss and does not get anywhere, then you should seriously think about how to reduce the risk.

Are you a day trader and you work with a 5-minute chart and your position is after 30 minutes (6 Candles) still in the loss, then you should think about the latest here to minimize risk.

A good measure is **to set the initial stop closer to the current market**. By doing this, you risk of course, that the stop is reached by the market, but the loss will be smaller. If the market afterwards moves in the desired direction, then you still have done the right thing. If the market does not do this and gets your stop out, then you also have done the right thing here. You have a loss, but at least you have done everything possible to minimize this loss. I call this active stop management.

A trader, who is playing his own game, is practicing active stop management. He does not wait until he is the victim of a volatile counter-movement of the market. He says: up to here and no further.

The second way to minimize risk is **to reduce the position itself**. This is possible in most cases. If you trade stocks, you sell half or a third of your shares. If you trade Forex, you can close half of the position. The measure does not work if you are trading futures and your position is just only one lot (1 contract). You cannot split one contract.

This is the reason why some traders have the opinion (and I share this opinion) that traders who trade only with a single contract are trading suboptimal. They restrict themselves in their action.

If you operate swing trading using the 4-hour chart, and bought, for example, two mini DAX futures, you can sell one of them, should your position not be in the profit after 24 hours.

When a position after a certain period does not exceed the breakeven point, this simply means that your assumption about future market development was wrong. No more, no less. Even if you did a thorough analysis of the market, you should know that your entry is always subject to random changes. Accordingly, your stop is also subject to random changes.

Why should the "market" just when you bought it, start to rise? That is an arrogant not to say megalomaniacal opinion, isn't it. As 'if the whole world was waiting at you to buy at last, so that the move can start.

The truth is that in the stock market you trade in a random walk. At any time, anything can happen (and the opposite). Get this clear and you will finally understand that it simply is a childlike wish that your analysis is correct and the market must comply with it.

In addition, that is why as a trader you should develop clear rules how you will manage the risk. You decide when you buy and sell. If you do not do this, the market activity will drive you astray, and you will eventually no longer understand the world. Believe me; I really speak from my own experience.

AND LET YOUR PROFITS RUN

So far, we have discussed the first part of the golden trading rule: cut your losses. Now, there is also a second part: and let your profits run. Here, I think that many traders do not really listen. I repeat the rule: let your profits run!

In other words, if we with respect to the first part of the rule should do every effort to minimize our losses, we must regarding the second part make every effort to ensure that we let our profits run.

If with respect to the losses I am extremely rigorous and close a losing position better today than tomorrow, I am utmost patient and generous about my winning positions. You read that right: generous and patient.

Why?

The breakeven point is for me like a kind of magic limit. Moreover, I am sure every trader knows this limit. As long as a position is under water, I feel uncomfortable. I do not like it, because I know that I am losing money and the longer I wait, the more I lose. Therefore, I am strict concerning my loss positions.

However, as soon as the position passes over the breakeven point, I start to relax. I know: This investment begins to pay off. However, I am still not calm because the position is still in the risk. While the direction of the trade seems to be right, I know that the market can turn at any time, and my position can turn in the loss again.

Nevertheless, it belongs also to the good trading habits that once a position becomes profitable, I start to reduce the risk. I will begin to push the stop-loss order in the direction of the breakeven point. In other words, the cumulative gains makes it possible to minimize the risk.

As an example, we can take a long position in the Dow Jones. Suppose you are a swing trader and bought the Dow Jones at 17,000 points. Your initial stop is 200 points lower at 16,800. Now suppose the Dow rises 17,100, it makes no sense to me to leave the stop at 16,800. In this case, I will set the stop at 16,900 (notwithstanding any chart technical considerations). I put my stop there because that is my rule. Do you understand?

If the Dow now continues to rise up to 17,200, then I am in the comfortable position to put my stop on breakeven, so at 17,000. This is the best of all worlds. For now, I have a profitable position that cannot walk in the loss again. Thus, I can sit back and watch the further development of the trade. Alternatively, in the language of the golden trading rule: letting my profits run.

That is also what some call a "free trade". This means that you only can win. The worst thing that can happen to you is that the market comes back and triggers the stop order. In this case, you would have gained nothing but lost nothing either.

Now, I have said before that I am generous in terms of winning positions. I stay patiently with the market and give it the space to develop. This does not mean that I have no rules on winning trades; I am just not as rigorous as in losing trades. Many traders unfortunately do the opposite: they are rigorous in winning trades (take profits once they appear) and are infinitely patient with losing positions.

Therefore, I am trying to do the exact opposite, which is also within the meaning of the golden rule, and within the meaning of my purse.

Regarding the management of profitable trades, I distinguish between trades with clearly defined price targets and trades that rely on larger movements (trend trades). This distinction is important, as it assumes a different stop management.

STOP MANAGEMENT IN TRENDING MARKETS

If you expect a larger move or the continuation of a larger trend, then you obviously want to get the most out of the trade. The classic type of stop-reduction in a trending market is to place the stop in each case under the last swing low. This measure is based on the **Dow Theory**, stating that a trend is characterized by higher highs and higher lows.

This approach initially seems logical. The trader hereby secures the accrued profits by a kind of manual trailing stop. Unfortunately, this method is also not free of errors, which is shown in the example in the E-Mini (S&P500 future) below.

E-Mini, 4-hour chart, Heikin Ashi

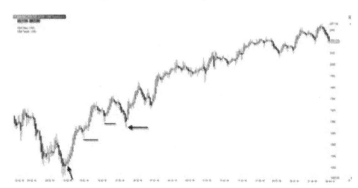

Suppose after the double bottom in the S&P500 from the beginning of 2016, the trader would have entered a long entry (arrow). His initial stop would thus, lie at the opening of the position slightly below the lows of the double bottom. The market begins actually to rise and after 13 white candles there is a first consolidation, which lasts only briefly. The market continues to rise after a few hours.

The trader uses the low of this consolidation to secure his profits and now pushes his stop up under this swing low (first horizontal line below). The market rises 9 candles higher and the next phase of consolidation occurs. The trader waits for it and after the market rises again, he pushes his stop again at the last low of this consolidation (second horizontal line).

The market rises again, but after seven white candles, it gets into a consolidation that lasts longer this time, and goes even lower than the previous one. The result is that the stop of the trader is triggered and thus the position is out of the market (horizontal arrow). Shortly after this happened, the market rises again and after eleven white candles reaches a new high.

Finally, in the following days and weeks the market continues to rise, and all the trader makes is the experience on how he missed huge profits, although his judgment in regard to the market direction was right and he had a position from the beginning of the move. He was thrown out of the market only by a short, temporary correction, which was not even a retracement.

Many traders have this experience. Their analysis is correct, they do the right thing by setting up a position, but they fail on risk management. With the classic recommendation "move the stop on the last respective swing low" to you, won´t get far in today's markets. Too many fakes always bring the stops out of the market. The smart money knows too well, of course, that trend followers use to place their stops at the swing lows. In addition, it is just too tempting to get these quickly.

In my experience, the cause of the whole problem of the stop reduction in trending markets lies in a wrong way of thinking, how to trade these markets. It is known that strong trends are interrupted from time to time by sharp corrections.

If you use this antiquated method of stop-reduction, you will see repeatedly that the market will get your stop out. Therefore, you will be stopped out at the worst point in the trend, although the trend is not over yet.

If you expect a larger movement and are positioned correctly, you should instead give the market space to really develop. As I am rigorous as long as my position stays in the loss, (I lose money!), I am also generous, once the position is in profit, (I make money!).

Why in God's name, will you cut the full development of your winning positions in good trends by tight stops? Can someone explain to me the purpose of this measure? If the second part of the golden trading rule is "let your profits run", then you should do this. As a swing trader, you can pocket fabulous profits with a very manageable risk. That is precisely the advantage of this trading style.

The argument of the opponents of this philosophy I know very well. They will say: If the trader would not have set the stop just below the last swing low of the upward movement, he might have risked that the upward movement would have been nullified by the market. He would therefore emit any accrued profits again and thus even risked a loss.

This argument is not to be easily dismissed. This scenario could occur, in fact, and it will happen now and again. However, it is known that most traders are more afraid; to give accrued gains back to the market, as to realize actual losses with a position.

In addition, it is precisely this fear that tempts them either to take profits quickly once a little of it is there, or to let the stop very closely follow the current price. As if they are not confident that their winning positions could continue to evolve. This is not rational behavior.

My argument is: every now and then the market come back, and the traders experience the accrued gains given back to the market. That is part of the game you play with yourself. Nevertheless, you will give away quite often very high profits by letting you stop too early, as it was the case in the example of the E-mini.

In other words: The lost profits are usually much higher than the occasional profits given back in case of a relapse of the market. If the trader goes for trends, the he should do it right.

To say it with a bon mot of the memorable Hungarian investor André Kostolany: "If pork, then it must drip - and if stock market, then it must be worth it."

I repeat it again. I am pedantic and rigorous when it comes to losses, but I am generous like a grandmother with her grandchildren, when it comes to profits.

Thus, the breakeven point is the magic border where I am either relaxing (in case of a gain) or get nervous (in case of a loss). When I am in profit again, my patience is almost endless (almost!). However, as long as I am in the loss, I am the most impatient person in the world. Most traders behave - sorry - just the opposite.

However, there is a second border after the breakeven point, which is even more important: **the break-even threshold**. As soon as I can set the stop to breakeven, I relax totally, because I cannot lose anymore. This threshold should be your primary goal as a swing trader. Then, the fun can begin.

Anything before the break-even threshold feels like work and strict risk management and that, it really is. What comes next is the state, which is why we love the stock market. We have a position at the right time in the right market and can watch now how this position makes money with increasing time. Isn´t that awesome?

Should in case of such winning positions in trending markets the trader not do any type of gain protection? Of course, he should operate a form of gain protection and eventually he must realize his profits. It is even very important that he eventually learn to say "thank you" and then make it out of the dust.

However, first, I just wanted initially to tell the trader the irrational fear of giving back any accrued gain. It will occasionally happen, and you cannot avoid it. It is in my view much worse, if you are stopped out early as in the image 2, and then have to watch that all the others are at the party but you.

I want you to put so to say in a kind grandmother- grandchild mood and appeal at your own generosity. Just give any winning position the air it needs to breathe. Make sure that you can put the stop to break even as quickly as possible, then nothing can happen to you anymore and you can go into a more observation mode.

What do I mean by that? Every trend has its own dynamics and internal logic. You can set the stop slightly higher if your position has a nice gain. There is nothing wrong, but do not set the stop at the last swing low. You might choose the penultimate swing low. If this is taken out of the market, then there is something wrong with this trend. Then you should be careful, or maybe close the position. You can buy it back at any time, if you are convinced that the trend is not over. In addition, here, nothing is forbidden.

An alternative would be to use a kind of trailing stop. This could be an ordinary trailing stop as in the example with the Dow Jones. In that case, I had used a trailing stop, which follows the price at a distance of 200 points. I recommend though choosing this trailing stop generously.

Figure 3: E-mini, 4-hour chart, Heikin Ashi

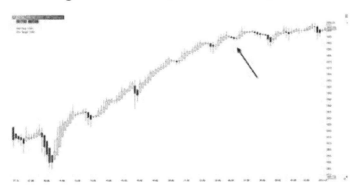

Figure 3, which is also from the S&P500, is an example from 2014. We see a very strong uptrend. The Heikin Ashi candles are at each upward movement invariably white and consolidation periods (usually after market closing) are short and almost insignificant. The first four buying waves are absolutely convincing. In such a case, you can confidently sit back and enjoy the ride.

The fifth purchase wave though (arrow) is no longer so convincing. After four white candles, several black candles arise and at the wave, this happens again. The trend is clearly out of breath. This is the phase in which I would recommend a trailing stop. It is the final phase of the trend, and it should be clear to you as a trader, that at any time a proper correction could occur.

In this example, the traders who had a long position were even lucky, because, after the market had reached its top, he kept going sideways on a very high level. With increasing duration, I would set the trailing stop ever closer. Initially still 30 points, but then soon I would go to 20 and even 10. Eventually your order will be executed and you are out of the market.

I hope that you understand the intention. In the final stage of a trend it is always about how to drive the harvest safely in the barn. You deserve it. You will be rewarded for your patience.

You get this harvest of course only when during the accumulation phase (the beginning of the trend) and in the momentum phase (here the trend is strongest, the candles are the biggest) you have set your stop at a generous distance from the current market. It makes no sense to try to follow a strong trend closely with a stop. Let it run!

Also, do not try to guess the high of the trend; you will not succeed as a rule. It is better to have clear stop-rules so that you get the best out of each trade. This will certainly not always succeed, but now and then, you might have a home run. Moreover, this does just fine to your account.

STOP-MANAGEMENT WITH PRICE TARGETS

When I work with a clear price target, for example, if I trade a range market, then it makes little sense in my eyes to work with a trailing stop. Just look at the example below in the EUR/USD.

Figure 4: EUR/USD, 1-hour chart

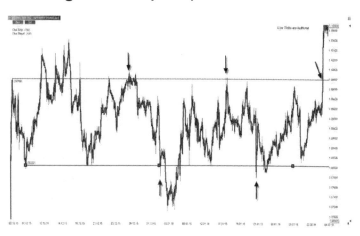

A range then becomes visible when the two delimiting lines have at least two significant touches. Only then, can the trader identify the range and trade it as such. In this case, five trades were possible. Three short trades (arrows above) and two long trades (arrows below).

It is the nature of a sideways market that the market players agree more or less on the current price. Of course, there are still fluctuations, which can be exploited by skillful range traders. In this case, I could see a range in the EUR/USD, which was broadly about 180 pips. As you can see, there were also several fakes and even a downright false downside breakout. Nevertheless, the market returned to the range.

Unlike trending markets, range markets are uncertain markets. You see this with a simple look at the chart. The price seems to shoot without any clear direction, like Ping-Pong balls back and forth. Here, to work with a trailing- Stop does not make sense in my eyes.

The price target at range trading is the respective opposite range limit. If you buy the support (bottom line), then your target automatically is the upper limit, so the resistance (upper horizontal line). You can make a maximum of 180 points gain in this example.

As a range trader, you assume that the support will hold, if you go long. Therefore, the stop should not be set too generous. I recommend here half of the range, i.e. 90 pips. As you can see, this measure would have worked well in the first two short trades. It would not have worked at the first long trade. Here the stop would have been the victim of market volatility.

The second long trade (bottom right arrow) reached very well the target price. However, look at the course antics that it took the EUR/USD until the target was reached. This is quite typical for a range market. For this reason you should not use a trailing stop here.

First, the euro shot up to half of the range high (i.e., the long position was already 90 pips in profit) and then returned all the way back to the entry point to fall below even. This is particularly annoying, but it does happen. If you had put here your stop prematurely at break-even, you would have been left behind.

I recommend thoroughly shortening the initial stop a bit at 45 pips, if you are already 90 pips in profit. The measures, which are right for trend markets, just do not apply to range markets. The trading of range markets is more than anything else a probability game. Some trades reach the target, others are stopped out.

In this example, we have the following result:

Three winning trades: 3 x 180 = 540 pips

Two losing trades: 2 x 90 = 180 pips

Total = 360 pips

THE FRANC TSUNAMI, A HEALING MOMENT OF THE TRADER COMMUNITY

Anyone wishing to enter Switzerland by crossing the border at the South German town of Konstanz on a Saturday afternoon and evening, often experiences a big surprise. A kilometer long queue is formed in front of the Swiss border. Who looks at the license plates, notes that it is not the Germans who want to enter Switzerland, but the Swiss! Has an invasion occurred here?

On Friday afternoons and Saturdays, it really looks as if this happened indeed, but the Swiss invaders bring to the German retailers a second Christmas Business, because since the spectacular rise of the Swiss franc on 15th January 2015, the shopping tourism has increased massively.

Not enough that the Swiss with their strong franc empty the supermarket shelves of the German border towns. They also wait until the forms for VAT refund will be printed. At the customs, they even get VAT back. Therefore, they win twice.

The event that is known in the stock market history as the Franc Tsunami, took place on 15th January 2015. Just a few days before 15th January, the Swiss National Bank had announced that it would do its utmost to defend the peg of 1.20 for the currency pair EUR/CHF imposed by themselves.

A few days later they did, which no one expected. They dropped the peg. The euro crashed within half an hour at around 15%. With a blow, all Swiss possessed 15% more purchasing power.

What is good for the Swiss shopping tourists and for the South German retailers, in my eyes is good for the trader community. The franc shock was actually the best thing that could happen to the traders. Although it has many quite evil, in some cases with legal repercussions. In addition, although some brokers did not survive the event, I still am glad that it happened.

One can regard the franc shock as a chapter in the "war of currencies" and it certainly is. We know now, at least since January 15th, that we may not believe any major player in the financial markets, and certainly not central bankers.

Many traders held a long position in the EUR/CHF in January 2015 because in the days before 15th January the price was just over 1.20. Since the Swiss National Bank, "guaranteed" the lower limit a long position seemed only logical and was regarded as a free trade.

As then, the unthinkable happened, some had perhaps placed a stop loss order at 1.19 or 1.18. Just in case. This helped them in no way, because the slippage (worse execution rates) was so great that the EUR/CHF fell within the shortest time from 1.20 to 0.85. The actual execution price of the stops was then in some cases at 0.85, which led to huge losses. Traders who had relied on the SNB (Swiss National Bank) partly lost six-figure sums.

In other words: In this extreme case, which is also called a **"Black Swan"**, the stop-loss order is useless. Although Black Swans are very rare. It is possible that every trader throughout his trading career could at least once become the victim of such an event.

A similar incident, though less dramatic occurred on 11th September 2001. After the attacks on the World Trade Center, the stock markets in the USA remained closed for days. No trader could liquidate his positions. Of course, the prices were, when the markets were reopened, considerably lower.

Healing the Franc Tsunami was in my eyes even to think seriously about the issue of position size. If private traders ever get the opportunity to see how a professional asset management works, they often wonder "how small" the positions are that are held or traded. Small in comparison to the existing capital of course.

With the exception of some hedge funds (of the kind George Soros), it is a rule with institutional investors that no single position may put the fund in trouble. Suppose a fund would have a position in stock XYZ, and this company goes bankrupt overnight. The share falls to zero, which is a total loss. You will often experience that this loss might represent a loss of 1 or 2% in the total balance of the fund. I would say this is a regrettable individual case, but it does not drive the fund into bankruptcy.

Private traders on the other hand often hold positions that exceed the value of their trading capital by far. Whoever has US $10,000 available to trade and purchases one mini lot on the EUR/USD (value US $ 10,000) has already invested his entire capital. Of course, the trader can buy much larger positions due to the high advantage in the forex markets. However, the question is whether he should do so.

The Franc Tsunami has yet demonstrated to us how dangerous it can be to keep positions that represent a multiple of the equity. If it goes wrong, as in the case of the Swiss franc shock, there is no representative of the federal government who comes to the microphone and secures the forex traders the full support of the taxpayer, sorry.

Therefore, as a private trader, you should ask yourself seriously the question of whether you should ever trade with leverage at all, although some brokers might offer you a leverage of 1:100 (some brokers 1: 400!). It seems tempting to trade a small capital of a few thousand US dollars in the shortest time to several millions. The much greater likelihood is that you will destroy this tiny capital within a few months if you are using leverage.

My recommendation to trade with small position sizes is based on the observation that most traders overestimate what they can achieve in a short period of time (a week or a month).

However, they underestimate what they can achieve within a longer period if you trade your strategy in a disciplined way over a period of 5 to 10 years.

It does seem fun when you can end your trading day and you have US$ 1,000 more in your account (if you have only a trading capital of US$ 10,000, for example). Nevertheless, can you do this every day?

In my view, it makes much more sense to treat your trading business actually like a real business. Meaning to start small and to trade only gradually with larger positions provided you are in a position to multiply your existing capital.

Do not try therefore to make your living by trading. This goal puts you under a lot of pressure. The danger then is that you are trading heavily leveraged and disproportionately take on high risks. As a rule, that is not good for most beginner traders.

It is much smarter to start very small (to trade, for example, in the Forex with Microlots, not with Minilots!) and to use no leverage at all, but with experience to increase gradually the positions. This will put you at the beginning under less pressure and you could transition calmly into the trading business.

The actual leverage is then in time. Most traders underestimate what they can achieve in a period of 5 or 10 years. In 5 years, you may be able to do things to which you are not yet in a position today. Give yourself the time to grow into this.

The relaxed trading with the smallest positions also has another positive effect. You can afford to work with more generous stop orders. Just as a swing trader, you should not put your stops too tight. Give the market some time to develop. If he does not do this after a set period, then you should seriously think about minimizing the risk as discussed earlier.

HOW MANY POSITIONS CAN I HOLD AT THE SAME TIME?

Certainly, as a swing trader you have the luxury that you do not have to constantly monitor your trades, which, for example, day traders or scalpers should do. You are in the comfortable position that you place your orders in the market and then you are able to leave. Since your position is provided both with a stop-loss as a take profit order, ultimately the market decides, which one of two orders will be executed first.

This puts you in the course capable of holding several positions simultaneously. Nevertheless, I would want to warn about doing this. I myself usually do not hold more than two positions simultaneously.

Why?

Today's markets are highly correlated. If something happens with the dollar typically this might have an impact on the stock market and for commodities certainly. Is there a strong move in the oil market, also, this is not without consequences for the stock market and for a whole range of commodity currencies, including the dollar.

In other words, if you hold, for instance, a position in the EUR/USD, in crude oil and in the Dow Jones, it could happen by an event in one of those markets that all others are affected. If you stand on the wrong side, it could happen that you may experience a loss in all three positions.

More importantly, there is also a more psychological component. When traders hold too many positions at the same time, they develop a certain indifference to certain positions. You may not manage all those positions with the same care that you would otherwise manage a single position. Keep it therefore rather simple and try to trade those markets in which you recognize a real chance. Less is often more.

GLOSSARY

Black Swan: Very rare event with great impact.

Breakeven: Point at which total cost and total revenue are equal.

Correlation: Correlation is a statistical measure of how two securities move in relation to each other.

Day trading: Day trading describes the speculative short-term trading in securities. A trader will open a position and within the same trading day close it again.

Drawdown: Drawdown is the maximum cumulative loss within a respective period and is presented usually as a percentage.

Dow Theory: The Dow Theory is the basis of all technical analysis of financial markets.

E-Mini Futures: Futures contract on the American index SP500.

Exit Strategy: A strategy that determines the exit from a market.

Forex: Forex Exchange Market, international foreign exchange market.

Guaranteed stop loss order: With this order, the broker guarantees to close the position exactly to the desired price.

Heikin Ashi chart: "Balancing on one foot" Japanese representation form of price changes.

Hit rate: The hit ratio is the ratio of winning trades to losing trades.

Initial Stop: The initial stop-loss limits the risk of a position at the moment of execution.

Long Position: To be long means to have purchased securities and thus own them.

Lot: A lot is the trading unit at the foreign exchange (Forex) and futures markets.

Microlot: A microlot corresponds to a contract of $ 1,000 in a currency pair.

Mini lot: A mini lot corresponds to a contract over $ 10,000 in a currency pair.

Momentum: The momentum informs the investor about the pace and strength of a price movement.

Pip: Percentage in point, the smallest change in the price in currency trading.

Range: A clear defined trading range over a given period.

Resistance: Price level at which increased sellers emerge.

Retracement: A temporary reversal that goes against the prevailing trend.

Scalping: Trading technique by which the trader trades minimal movements in the market.

Short position: A trader is short when he sells a position without owning them (short sale).

Slippage: The difference between the estimated and the actual price of an asset at the execution.

Stop loss order: Sell order, which is carried out once a certain price is reached.

Trailing stop: Automatic stop loss order, which follows the price at a set distance.

Support: Price level at which buyers increasingly emerge.

Trend following: Trading strategy, which focuses on the following of a once identified trend.

Volatility: Standard deviation. Specifies how the price of a market varies.

OTHER BOOKS BY HEIKIN ASHI TRADER

How to start a Trading Business with $500

Many new traders have little capital available in the beginning, but this is not an obstacle to starting a trading career anyway.

However, this book is not about how to grow a $500 account into a $500,000 account. It is precisely these exaggerated return expectations that bring most beginners to failure.

Instead, the author shows, in a realistic way, how you can become a full-time trader in spite of limited start-up capital. This applies both for traders who want to remain private, as well as for those who want to eventually trade customer funds.

This book shows step by step how to do it. In addition, there is a concrete action plan for each step. Anyone can be a trader in principle, if he or she is willing to learn how this business works.

Table of Contents

How to Scalp the Mini DAX Futures?

Thanks to the introduction of the Mini-DAX futures (FDXM) private traders with smaller accounts are afforded the opportunity to scalp the German DAX Index to professional terms. Unlike most other trading instruments, Futures are the most transparent and effective way to make money in the financial markets.

Scalpers have infinitely more trading opportunities than position traders or day traders, which constitutes the real strength of this trading style. A scalper may therefore manage his capital much more effectively than all other market participants and thus achieve much greater returns than would otherwise be the case.

The Heikin Ashi Trader shows in this book how to successfully scalp this new future on the DAX. You will learn how to enter the market, how to manage your position and at which point you should back out. In addition, the book contains a wealth of tips and tools to make your trading even more effective and precise.

Table of Contents

ABOUT THE AUTHOR

Heikin Ashi Trader is the pen name of a trader who has more than 15 years of experience in day trading futures and foreign exchange. He specializes in scalping and fast day trading. In addition to this, he has published multiple self-explanatory books on his trading activities. Popular topics are on: scalping, swing trading, money- and risk management.

IMPRINT

Texts: © Copyright by Heikin Ashi Trader

Swiss Post Box 106287

Zürcher Strasse 161

CH-8010 Zürich

Switzerland

94524324R00043

Made in the USA
Columbia, SC
25 April 2018